How to Cook Outdoors

MONTGOMERY WARD AND COMPANY, INC.

CHICAGO 7, ILLINOIS

How to Use
This Barbecue Book

The instructions and recipes in this book have been designed and developed to use as a quick and easy reference while barbecuing. So, before you start to barbecue, read the general instructions on pages 4 to 8. Also, see special instructions for grill and spit barbecuing on pages 9 and 31 to 37 respectively. Then, when you are familiar with these directions, have fun trying the recipes.

GRILL BARBECUING

For those "spur-of-the-moment" picnics, grill barbecuing is the answer. Easy and quick-to-cook, juicy individual steaks, hot dogs, hamburgers or seafood such as shrimp or clams, are ready to serve right from the grill in a matter of minutes. The section on Grill Barbecuing starts on page 9.

SPIT BARBECUING

Spit barbecuing is amazingly easy and can be even more fun than grill barbecuing. First, read the general instructions for spit barbecuing starting on page 31. Then, prepare the special recipes which follow and watch the food take on a luscious golden-brown color. Sniff those tempting aromas and decide for yourself which recipes are your favorites!

SMOKING

After learning to spit barbecue, the next step is smoking. Read pages 48 and 49, and you will have opened the door to a whole new phase of barbecuing.

BARBECUE EXTRAS

Remember also that you should plan a well rounded meal. This can be a simple, carefree task. While barbecuing meat, fish or poultry, you can grill other foods at the same time to serve with it. In the section from pages 50 to 59, you will find the outdoor "know-how" for barbecuing vegetables, fruits and hot breads. Salads and dessert suggestions are also included.

Sauces, marinades and glazes are on pages 60 to 62. It is easy to refer to them—just flip to the back of the book.

Use this book as a guide. Improvise and experiment with your own creative ideas for the utmost in barbecuing pleasure.

Where to find it

Description of Equipment

This section is to help you identify your equipment and learn its proper use and care.

BARBECUE BRAZIER

The bowl type unit is called a brazier and consists of a fire bowl mounted on three legs. Grill barbecuing is done on a wire rack called a grill . The grill is raised and lowered by means of a crank which moves a tongue and in turn moves the raiser rod which iş in the center tube of the fire bowl. Better braziers are equipped with a hood which protects the fire and food from the wind and permits barbecuing on the spit.

BARBECUE WAGON

The box-type unit is called a barbecue wagon and consists of a body and hood with a reflector. Grill barbecuing is done on wire racks called grills . In this unit the fire is held in a fire pan which is adjusted by means of a crank which controls the raise and lower arms holding the fire pan.

BARBECUE SPIT

The barbecue spit is the device used for rotisserie cooking. This is called spit cooking by the barbecue chef. The barbecue spit is a metal shaft or rod which is pointed at one end to permit easy insertion into meats. Most spit rods have a wooden handle on the other end. A notch in the shaft near the handle is called a spit rod bearing. Wire skewers called spit forks are placed on the spit rod to hold the meat in position. These spit forks are made secure by tightening the wing screws . The pointed end of the spit rod is inserted into the spit crank or spit motor and the spit rod bearing is placed on the gravity slot or groove

Read This Before You Light a Fire – You'll be Glad You Did!

A layer of porous material in the fire bowl or fire pan of your unit is a most important aid to good barbecuing. This base provides the proper bed on which to build your fire.

Four Important Reasons for Using a Base

1 The base protects the fire bowl or fire pan from the heat and thus prolongs the life of the barbecue unit.

2 The base allows air to circulate around the fuel, enabling it to burn uniformly.

3 The base retains and reflects heat. This reduces fuel costs and also provides more even heat distribution.

4 The base absorbs fats as they drip from the hot food, lessening flameups. It also traps ash as it falls from the briquets.

What to Use for a Base? How Deep Should It Be?

The base material should be clean, crushed stones, blue stones or pea gravel. The best size to use is about 1/4 to 3/8 inch in diameter. You can also use volcanic ash. Whichever base you choose, be sure that you have enough to fill your particular barbecue unit. Directions for filling follow:

FIRE BOWL

Fill the fire bowl with one of the base materials mentioned above. Use enough base so that it is about 1/2 inch from the top of the center tube and level out to the very edge of the fire bowl.

For spit barbecuing on braziers, with an adjustable air draft in the fire bowl, fill the rear half of the bowl with gravel, using the separator to hold back the gravel. When starting the fire, place briquets over the draft. After fire is started, lift briquets onto the gravel toward the rear.

FIRE PAN

Fill the fire pan with the base material. It should be 1/2 to 3/4 inch deep in the pan.

For most efficient use of the gravel base, air spaces must not become filled with ash or fat drippings. You can either replace the gravel or clean it by one of these three methods. Be sure gravel is dry before using.

1 Sift ash from the gravel through heavy wire mesh. If necessary, wash to remove fat accumulations.

2 Wash in a pail of hot sudsy water. Spread out to dry thoroughly.

3 Spread out on a cement surface and spray with a garden hose.

Fuel for the Fire

A great many brands of fuel are sold for barbecuing; however use only a good grade of charcoal or charcoal briquets made from hardwoods. We recommend charcoal briquets because they are uniform in size, give a steady, long-lasting fire and are most economical. They give off very little smoke and odor because they contain only a trifling amount of resin. Charcoal briquets give the true, much-sought-after charcoal flavor. Other fuels, such as soft wood charcoals, fail to produce a steady heat, burn either too fast or too slow and have a high resin content which imparts an undesirable taste to delicately flavored foods.

Charcoal briquets, long the favorite fuel of the country's best chefs, are pure charcoal made from a variety of hardwoods. This charcoal has been ground to a powder and mixed with a binder of water and cornstarch. The mixture is then compressed into briquets.

Charcoal briquets have been used in testing all the recipes in this book.

Four Important Accessories to Handle Fire

Fire Rake   To arrange gravel and group the briquets (moving them from one place to another). Don't be without one!

Pair of Fire Tongs   To pick up single briquets, to arrange the fire and handle foil-wrapped packages of food. A most useful tool!

Shovel   To shovel briquets when arranging fire. Use it for gravel; knock the ash off the briquets with it. A barbecue shovel is something every barbecuer will find absolutely necessary!

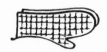

Barbecue Mitts   To protect your hands from the heat of the briquets and permit you to safely handle hot tools, equipment and dishes. Get a pair of heavy, asbestos barbecue mitts — they are wonderful!

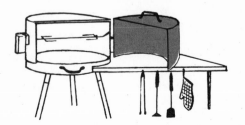

To Start a Barbecue Fire

Start your fire early—this is the key point. Allow time for the briquets to become completely covered with gray ash. Length of time depends on the starter you use.

Start Your Fire in 1 of These 3 Easy Ways

WARD'S LIQUID LIGHTER

Put a mound of briquets about 10 inches in diameter and 5 inches high on the gravel. Follow instructions on the can for pouring liquid over the briquets and lighting them. The fire will be ready in 30 to 45 minutes. Never squirt more liquid lighter on a lighted fire.

STAR-STYX

Put a mound of briquets about 10 inches in diameter and 5 inches high on the gravel. Insert pieces of Star-Styx and light as directed on the package. The fire will be ready in 20 to 25 minutes.

ELECTRIC STARTER

Put a mound of briquets about 10 inches in diameter and 2 or 3 briquets high on the gravel, with the top of the mound flat. Plug the starter into an electric outlet and place on briquets for 5 to 7 minutes until briquets ignite. Then move the starter to another area or remove it and let the fire spread naturally. Your fire will be ready in 10 to 15 minutes.

Watch the Fire Grow

Briquets ignite in small areas which appear as gray spots. These spots enlarge until they cover the entire briquet. When the briquets are entirely covered with gray ash, they are ready to use. However, the ash acts as an insulator. In order to take full advantage of their heat, tap the briquets occasionally to knock off the ash.

Before Adding Briquets to a Fire   Place extra ones on the gravel near the fire to warm them before using them on the fire.

To Put the Fire Out

Remove briquets with a shovel or fire tongs; drop into a pail of water. After soaking them a few minutes, pour off the water and let the briquets dry. Use them for your next barbecue, but not for starting the fire, as they may be difficult to light. Start the fire with new briquets. Warm up partially used ones, then add them. This is real economy!

Timing Your Barbecue

Variables affect the length of time required to barbecue. Keep them in mind whenever you barbecue and estimate the time accordingly.

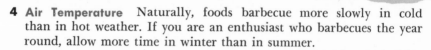

1 Fuel   A good grade of fuel always burns at a constant rate and makes a hotter fire. Poor quality fuels cannot be depended upon for the same heat intensity each time you barbecue because the burning rates are not uniform.

2 Quantity of Briquets   Burning briquets closely spaced or heaped high hasten barbecuing time. Use fewer briquets for slower cooking.

3 Distance from Fire   The farther the meat is from the fire, the longer the barbecuing time.

4 Air Temperature   Naturally, foods barbecue more slowly in cold than in hot weather. If you are an enthusiast who barbecues the year round, allow more time in winter than in summer.

5 Humidity   Since briquets readily absorb moisture from the air, which makes them harder to ignite, be sure to store them in a dry place.

6 Weight and Type of Meat   Small pieces of meat or fowl will cook in less time than large roasts.

7 Temperature of Meat   Remove meat from freezer or refrigerator long enough ahead of barbecuing to allow it to come to room temperature.

8 Breeze Direction and Speed   Your fire may start more easily if the breeze blows directly into the unit. However, once you begin to barbecue, turn the back of the hood into the breeze. Breezes, especially while grilling, cool the top surface of the meat and carry away the heat.

9 Hood or Windshield   A hood or windshield on your barbecue unit reflects a great deal of heat, helps shorten barbecuing time and saves fuel. This feature is of particular value in chilly or breezy weather.

10 Ash Coating on Briquets   Knock the gray ash off the briquets in order to utilize all the available heat. The ash coating insulates the briquets and reduces their efficiency.

Care of Equipment

Always keep your equipment clean. Wash the wire grill immediately after using. Wash the hood and cutting board surfaces. Wash or replace the gravel frequently. Oil the wheels and axles frequently and keep the threads on the cranks oiled. Tighten nuts, screws and hub caps periodically.

Grill Barbecuing

When the briquets are completely covered with gray ash, they are ready to arrange for barbecuing. Use tongs or a rake for handling the fire. Barbecue mitts are also essential for safety.

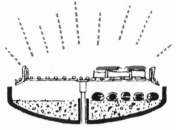

1 Spread the hot briquets in a single layer over the gravel, about 1/2 inch apart. This produces the most even heat and reduces flame-up caused by food drippings.

2 Have the fire cover an area slightly larger than that which will be covered by the food. When barbecuing small quantities of food on units having a Divided Grill, confine the fire to an area under half of the grill.

3 Always knock any remaining gray ash off the briquets before adjusting the height of the grill.

4 For general grill barbecuing, unless otherwise stated, adjust grill or fire pan so that the food is about 3 inches above the burning briquets.

5 In recipes which suggest that the meat be seared, first adjust the grill to the lowest possible position or the fire pan to the highest position. Sear for the specified time. Then, readjust the grill or fire pan as directed in the recipe.

6 Before grill barbecuing lean meats, rub the grill with cooking oil or a piece of fat.

7 Lean meats and poultry barbecued on the grill must be constantly basted and turned every 3 to 5 minutes. This prevents drying out and burning. Spareribs, chicken parts and lean meats should be barbecued at a higher level from the fire, and for a longer time, than steaks or chops.

8 Meats are barbecuing when juices appear on the uncooked surface, or when fat on the edge of meat, coming in contact with the grill, becomes translucent and juices bubble on the side of the fat.

9 To control the heat while grill barbecuing, you can either adjust the height of the grill or fire pan, or add or remove briquets as required, to get the desired amount of heat.

10 The use of nut or fruit wood sawdust or chips, such as hickory and cherry whets appetites with the wonderful aroma and imparts a wonderful new flavor to the grilled foods. Follow the instructions in the Smoking Section on pages 48 and 49.

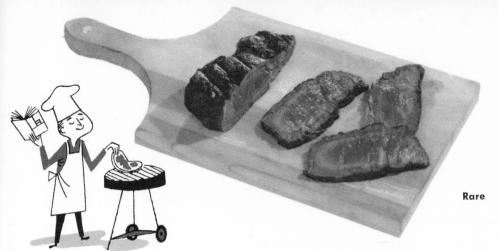

Steaks for the Grill

Steak is mighty fine eating, any time, any place. But when it is barbecued out-of-doors and comes sizzling hot from the grill, then steak is food fit for the gods.

What kind of steak shall it be? If you are not sure about your selection, have a small conference with your meat-man.

Good beef has a bright-red color, when fresh. If it has been aged, then the color is slightly purplish. However, most steaks have not been aged. There should be a generous edge of fat on the steak and it should be cream-colored, firm and flaky. In addition, good quality meat will be well marbled, flecked or streaked with fat.

The choice cuts to barbecue are porterhouse, sirloin, T-bone, club, rib, whole beef tenderloin or individual filet mignon.

Of course, you can also barbecue such cuts as flank steak and round steak. These, however, require a little different cooking procedure, carving technique or use of a tenderizer such as a marinade. Full instructions are given in the recipes for preparation of the meat.

Medium

10

Steak, rare, medium or well done? This is a debatable question. Of course, the final decision is yours, but we strongly suggest rare or medium-rare barbecuing for the finest flavor and texture.

The three steaks illustrated on page 10 and below, were all of the same thickness and color before barbecuing. Note that longer cooking changes the color and shrinks the meat. But there is more to the story than color and thickness. Flavor and texture are also changed. To determine whether or not a steak is done to your liking, make a small cut in the meat, near the bone.

Rare A rare steak is not a raw one. It is cooked just long enough to heat it thoroughly and take on a golden brown color. But when cut, the inside is bright red and the juices run freely.

Medium A medium-done steak has a deeper layer of brown and a good pink color in the center, but is not quite as juicy as a rare steak.

Well Done A well-done steak has lost all of its pink color. This steak has also lost most of its juices, is thinner and less tender.

For those who enjoy a good garlic flavor, cut a garlic clove in half and rub both sides of the steak with it. The strength of the flavor depends upon the amount you rub on the steak. For a delicate garlic flavor, throw a clove into the fire, under the grilling steak.

Some people prefer to sear a steak by putting it very close to the briquets for 2 or 3 minutes. This is a matter of individual taste and depends on whether or not you like a darker crusty surface.

Always turn a steak with a pair of tongs. Do not lose juices by carelessly puncturing the steak with a fork.

Season steak with salt and pepper after removing it from the grill. Or if preferred, season the cooked side immediately after turning.

Marinades help to tenderize cuts such as round steak and flank steak. Excellent marinade recipes will be found on page 60.

Well Done

Porterhouse Steak

Porterhouse steaks, cut 2 inches thick. Allow 3/4 to 1 pound per person.

Several cloves of garlic to put on the fire and a marinade, if desired (see page 60). Fat or cooking oil, salt and pepper.

Tongs for handling steak, cutting board, carving knife and fork.

HERE IS WHAT YOU DO

1 Marinate steak ahead of time.

2 Space hot briquets about 1/2 inch apart. Rub the grill with a piece of fat cut from the steak or cooking oil. Throw garlic on fire.

3 Lay steak on grill. Lower grill and sear steak 2 to 3 minutes. Then, raise grill 3 inches above briquets to barbecue steak.

4 When meat juices rise on the uncooked surface, turn the steak. A 2-inch steak cooked rare, requires about 10 to 15 minutes per side; cooked medium allow 15 to 20 minutes total searing and barbecuing time per side. Allow less time for a thinner steak and more time for a thicker steak.

5 Lower grill again. Sear second side of steak 2 to 3 minutes. Raise grill and continue to barbecue until done as desired.

6 Remove steak from grill and season with salt and pepper.

Steaks Galore

There are many steaks which make wonderful barbecue fare. Using the information below, select the steak which suits your needs. To barbecue, follow the general directions for Porterhouse Steak on the opposite page. Barbecuing time depends on the thickness and cut of the beef. Times below, are for 1½-inch thick steaks cooked rare. Allow a slightly longer time for medium- or well-done steaks. For thinner steaks, allow a little less time; for thicker steaks, allow a little longer time.

RIB STEAK

This steak has a single bone along one side. Allow 1 rib steak per person, cut at least 1½ inches thick. Barbecue 6 to 8 minutes per side.

CLUB STEAK

This small steak has little or no bone. Allow 1 club steak per person. Have steaks cut at least 1½ inches thick. Barbecue 6 to 8 minutes per side.

T-BONE STEAK

The T-shaped bone in the center of the meat gives this steak its name. Have T-bone steaks cut at least 1½ inches thick. Allow 1/2 to 3/4 pound per person. Barbecue 6 to 8 minutes per side.

SIRLOIN STEAK

This steak has a pin-bone or wedge-bone in the meat. The wedge-bone sirloin is particularly suitable for serving a crowd. If it is cut 2 inches thick, it can easily be sliced for sandwiches. Have steak cut at least 1½ inches thick. Allow 1/3 to 3/4 pound per person. Barbecue 8 to 10 minutes per side.

TENDERLOIN OR FILLET OF BEEF

This boneless cut of meat is very tender and easy to carve. Rare, medium and well-done meat may be served from the same piece of meat. Barbecue a whole tenderloin 15 to 18 minutes per side turning once.

CHUCK STEAK

This less tender cut of beef is delicious when properly prepared. Have meat cut 3/4 to 1 inch thick. Allow 3/4 pound per person. Select one of the marinades on page 60. Marinate steak in refrigerator at least 6 hours. Drain meat and barbecue about 15 minutes per side; turn once.

Round Steak

HERE IS WHAT YOU NEED

Boneless beef round steaks having a generous edging of fat and cut about 1 inch thick. Allow about 1/2 pound per person.

Spiced Marinade, if desired (see page 60). Cooking oil, salt and pepper.

Tongs for handling the steak, cutting board, carving knife and fork.

HERE IS WHAT YOU DO

1 Marinate steak ahead of time with Spiced Marinade.

2 Space hot briquets about 1/2 inch apart.

3 Brush grill with cooking oil.

4 Lay steak on grill and barbecue about 3 inches above briquets.

5 When meat juices rise on the uncooked surface and edge of fat touching the grill becomes translucent, turn the steak. For steak 1 inch thick, allow about 12 minutes per side for rare, 16 minutes per side for medium and 20 minutes per side for well-done steak. Barbecue until done as desired.

6 Remove steak from grill and season with salt and pepper.

Flank Steak

HERE IS WHAT YOU NEED

Flank steak, having a generous portion of fat, about 3/4 inch thick. Allow about 1/2 pound per person.

Several cloves of garlic to put on fire, if desired. Cooking oil, melted butter or margarine, salt and pepper.

Small, sharp knife for scoring; tongs for turning and handling the steak, cutting board, carving knife and fork.

HERE IS WHAT YOU DO

1 With small knife score steak lightly, crisscross fashion, on both sides.

2 Space hot briquets about 1/2 inch apart. Throw garlic cloves on fire.

3 Rub grill with cooking oil.

4 Lay steak on grill and barbecue 1½ to 2 inches above briquets.

5 When juices rise on the uncooked surface, turn the steak. For steak 3/4 inch thick, allow 5 to 6 minutes per side. Steak should be rare in center. Barbecue until done.

6 Remove steak from grill and cut diagonally, across the grain, in very thin slices. Season with melted butter, salt and pepper.

Hot Dog Jamboree

Kids love hot dogs and parties. So, why not plan a hot dog barbecue party for the youngsters? And, since hot dogs need only to be heated through, let the kids barbecue their own. Here are a few pointers for planning the party.

Keep The Menu Simple. Have plenty of hot dogs, rolls and all the "fixings" plus ice cream, cookies and milk. Make your selection of "fixings" from the list which follows.

Relish (see page 62), pickle relish, mustard-relish, Mustard Butter (see page 53), prepared mustard, catchup, sliced cheese, beans, sauerkraut, peanut butter, sweet or dill pickles, slices of bacon to wrap around hot dogs and wooden picks to secure the bacon.

Plan Ahead. Have everything ready at party time to avoid confusion. Make a list of all the equipment you will need such as, extra tables for work space, barbecue tools, plates and cups. Remember, too, that you will need a can or basket for the rubbish.

Keep Them Busy. Plan to keep the youngsters busy helping or playing games. Be sure to give everyone a turn at the barbecue to avoid hurt feelings.

Cheeseburgers

HERE IS WHAT YOU NEED

Ground beef and sliced, processed American cheese. A pound of beef makes 4 to 6 patties. Allow one slice of cheese for each patty.

For each pound of meat allow 1 teaspoon salt, 1/4 teaspoon pepper; add 1 to 2 tablespoons minced onion, if desired. Hamburger rolls, catchup, prepared mustard and pickle relish to serve with cheeseburgers.

Spatula for turning.

HERE IS WHAT YOU DO

1 Mix beef with salt and pepper; add onion. Shape meat into thick patties.

2 Space hot briquets 1/2 inch apart.

3 Lay patties on grill 3 inches above briquets. Barbecue about 10 minutes; turn. Barbecue about 3 minutes longer. Top each patty with a slice of cheese and continue barbecuing until meat is done as desired and cheese melts. Barbecue a total of 16 minutes for medium-done cheeseburgers.

4 Serve on hamburger rolls with catchup or mustard and pickle relish.

Hamburgers Plain 'n' Fancy

Just "plain" hamburgers, sizzling hot from the charcoal fire, make mighty fine eating. But "fancy" hamburgers are good too. For a change of flavor before, during or after barbecuing hamburgers, we offer these suggestions.

FLAVOR IN THE MEAT

Add one of the following ingredients in a quantity to suit your taste.

1 Seasonings: Sweet basil, thyme, marjoram, sage, celery salt, chili powder.

2 Cheese: Crumbled blue cheese, grated Parmesan or Cheddar.

3 Sauces: Worcestershire, Tabasco, barbecue or chili sauce, mustard, horseradish.

4 Nuts: Chopped almonds, pecans, walnuts.

FLAVOR FROM THE FIRE

1 For a garlic flavor, put several garlic cloves on the fire.

2 For hickory smoked hamburgers, follow directions on pages 48 and 49.

FLAVOR ON THE BUNS

Garlic, Herb, Mustard, or Roquefort Butter see recipes on page 53.

IN-BETWEENS

Make very thin patties, allow 2 per serving. Spread one patty with prepared mustard; sprinkle with grated Cheddar cheese. Top with second patty and pinch edges to seal.

DOUBLEBURGERS

Make very thin patties, allow 2 per serving. Barbecue the patties. During the last few minutes of barbecuing, lay a thin slice of cheese on one of the hamburgers to make a cheeseburger. Put the plain hamburger on a toasted, split bun; spread with mayonnaise. Now pile, high as you like, with sliced onion, shredded lettuce and piccalilli. Top with cheeseburger; cover the whole stack with the remaining piece of bun.

WRAP-AROUNDS

Make hamburgers in the shape of frankfurters; wrap a slice of bacon around each; secure with wooden picks.

Lamb Steak

HERE IS WHAT YOU NEED

Lamb steaks, cut 1 inch thick. Allow 1 steak per person.

Marinate, if desired, with one of the Marinades from page 60. Salt and pepper for seasoning.

Tongs for turning and handling the steaks.

HERE IS WHAT YOU DO

1 Marinate steaks ahead of time.

2 Space hot briquets about 1/2 inch apart.

3 Lay steaks on grill and barbecue 2 to 3 inches above briquets.

4 When meat juices rise on the uncooked surface and fat, resting on the grill, becomes translucent and bubbles, turn the steaks. Allow about 12 minutes per side for medium and 15 minutes per side for well-done lamb steaks. Continue barbecuing until done as desired.

5 Remove steaks from grill and season with salt and pepper.

Kidney Lamb Chops

HERE IS WHAT YOU NEED

Kidney or English lamb chops, cut 2 inches thick. Allow 1 chop per person.

Cooking oil, hickory chips for smoking, if desired (see page 48); salt and pepper.

Tongs for turning and barbecue brush.

HERE IS WHAT YOU DO

1 Space hot briquets about 1/2 inch apart. Rub grill with cooking oil. Put 2 or 3 prepared hickory chips on the fire.

2 Lay chops on grill. Lower grill; sear chops 2 to 3 minutes. Then raise grill 3 inches above briquets to barbecue chops.

3 When meat juices rise on the uncooked surface, turn the chops. Allow 15 minutes total searing and barbecuing time per side for medium-done and 20 minutes per side for well-done chops. Lower grill; sear second side of chops 2 minutes. Raise grill; barbecue until done.

4 Remove from grill and season with salt and pepper.

Plan a buffet barbecue. Prepare a "help-yourself" platter made of Kidney Lamp Chops, individually wrapped servings of California Green Beans (see page 54) and Ginger-Mint Pears (see page 57).

Pork Chops

Loin pork chops — either rib, center-cut, or shoulder chops, cut 1 inch thick. Allow 2 chops per person.

Tangy Pineapple Glaze, if desired (see page 61).

Tongs for turning and barbecue brush.

1 Space hot briquets 1/2 inch apart.

2 Lay chops on grill and barbecue 2 to 3 inches above briquets.

3 Barbecue chops 15 to 20 minutes on each side, turning just once. Brush with Tangy Pineapple Glaze the last 10 minutes of barbecuing.

Barbecued Spareribs

Buy loin ribs. Allow 3/4 to 1 pound of ribs per person. Barbecue spareribs the same as Pork Chops, above, but turn ribs and brush with cooking oil every 2 to 3 minutes. Brush with Sweet-Sour Basting Sauce (see page 61) during the last 10 minutes of barbecuing. Allow 30 to 45 minutes total time. Meat pulls away from the bone when done.

Ham Steak

"Fully cooked" or "ready-to-eat" ham slice, cut $1\frac{1}{2}$ to 2 inches thick. Allow about 1/2 pound per person.

Tangy Pineapple Glaze, if desired (see page 61). Cooking oil.

Tongs for turning and barbecue brush.

1 If you have had steaks curl, slash fat edge at $1\frac{1}{2}$-inch intervals.

2 Space hot briquets about 1/2 inch apart. Rub grill with cooking oil.

3 Lay steak on grill and barbecue 2 to 3 inches above briquets.

4 Barbecue a $1\frac{1}{2}$-inch thick steak about 8 minutes per side; turn just once. Brush top with Tangy Pineapple Glaze during the last 5 minutes of barbecuing.

Chicken Halves

HERE IS WHAT YOU NEED

Broiler-fryer chickens, weighing 2 to 3½ pounds each. Have chickens cut in halves or quarters, as desired. Allow about 1/2 chicken per person.

Cooking oil, melted butter or margarine. Cranberry Glaze, if desired (see page 61).

Tongs for turning and barbecue brush.

HERE IS WHAT YOU DO

1 Rub chicken parts with cooking oil.

2 Space hot briquets 1/2 inch apart.

3 Lay chickens, cut-side down, on grill. Lower grill and sear the chickens about 3 minutes on each side. Raise grill 3 inches above briquets and continue to barbecue. Brush chickens with melted butter and turn frequently during barbecuing. Barbecue 25 to 35 minutes, depending on size. Wings pull away easily from body when chickens are done. Brush skin-side during last few minutes of barbecuing time with the Cranberry Glaze.

Liver and Bacon Roll-Ups

HERE IS WHAT YOU NEED

Center-cut calf or very young beef liver, sliced 1/4 inch thick plus lean, thick bacon slices. Allow 2 slices liver and 4 slices bacon per person.

Moist Bread Stuffing: Use a package of prepared bread stuffing and mix it according to directions on package. Melted butter, salt and pepper.

Wooden picks. Tongs for turning and handling liver.

HERE IS WHAT YOU DO

1 Prepare Moist Bread Stuffing, allowing 1 cup stuffing for 8 Roll-Ups.

2 Spread one side of each slice of liver with about 2 tablespoons stuffing and roll up from the small end. Wrap 2 slices of bacon tightly around each roll and secure with wooden picks. Brush with melted butter.

3 Space hot briquets about 1/2 inch apart.

4 Put Roll-Ups on grill and barbecue 2½ to 3 inches above the briquets.

5 Barbecue Roll-Ups until done, turning several times to brown evenly. Allow 20 to 25 minutes total barbecuing time. Liver may be served when pink inside. Avoid overcooking or drying out liver.

6 Remove from grill and season with salt and pepper.

Barbecued

Whether you're planning a barbecue for a crowd or just a few, why not have kebobs? First, count the skewers to make sure you'll have plenty to go 'round. Next, decide what meat to serve and marinate it ahead of time. Then, select and prepare a variety of vegetables and some fruits, if you like.

At the last minute, arrange the foods on platters. Put out bowls of a marinade, a basting sauce and a glaze. Then, relax — let everyone make his own combination!

Either alternate the foods on one skewer, as shown, or string each kind separately. Pack the food on tightly and barbecue, turning often. Tips on preparation of the foods and a couple of recipe suggestions follow to make your barbecue a success.

POINTS TO REMEMBER

1 Cut meat in 1- to 1½-inch cubes.

2 Use firm fruits and vegetables. If necessary, cut foods in different size pieces so all will be done at the same time.

3 Brush all kebobs with cooking oil, a marinade, sauce or glaze while barbecuing.

4 Grill kebobs over a hot fire; turn often.

MEATS AND SEAFOOD TO USE

Shoulder or leg of lamb; sirloin tip or round of beef; "fully cooked" ham; bologna; cubed luncheon meat or sausage; frankfurters; chicken livers. Shrimp, oysters or scallops, wrapped in bacon.

Kebobs

VEGETABLES AND FRUITS TO USE

Raw or cooked, sweet and white potatoes; red and green peppers; zucchini squash; small red or green tomatoes; small white onions; eggplant; mushroom caps; cucumbers.

Raw or cooked peaches; raw apples; raw, cooked or dried apricots; bananas; raw or canned pineapple chunks; unpeeled avocado; Maraschino cherries.

Lamb Kebobs

Cut **lamb** in 1-inch cubes and marinate in a marinade (see page 60). Cut stems off **large mushrooms;** peel caps, if necessary. Remove seeds from **red and green peppers** and cut in 2-inch pieces. Cut **narrow zucchini** in 1½-inch pieces. Leave **small tomatoes whole.**

Just before barbecuing, drain lamb; reserve the marinade. Thread lamb, squash, tomatoes, red and green peppers and mushrooms on skewers, as pictured. Brush with reserved marinade or cooking oil before and often during barbecuing. Barbecue about 3 inches above the briquets 15 to 20 minutes, or until lamb is done; turn frequently.

Ham Kebobs

Cut **"fully cooked" ham** in 1½-inch cubes. Thread the ham on skewers alternately with **canned pineapple chunks, Maraschino cherries** and **2-inch cubes of eggplant.** Brush with **Sweet-Sour Basting Sauce** (see page 61) before and during barbecuing. Barbecue kebobs 3 inches above briquets 6 to 8 minutes, or until eggplant is tender; turn often.

A-Hunting We Did Go!

If you are the barbecue chef with freshly bagged game, a freezer full of game, or one looking for interesting new foods to barbecue, try the recipes below and on pages 27, 40 and 41. Here are a few basic rules to follow for the care of your game.

1 Game should be cleaned and cooled as quickly as possible after shooting.

2 Generally speaking, game should be allowed to firm up or age, a few days to a few weeks, before cooking. The amount of time will depend on the game.

3 Bring all game to room temperature before barbecuing.

Rabbit

Follow basic rules above. Refrigerate rabbit about 2 days. Cut into serving-size pieces. Wrap a slice of bacon around each piece; secure with wooden picks. Brush with cooking oil or melted butter. Space briquets 1/2 inch apart. Lay meat on grill 3 inches above briquets and barbecue. Brush with melted butter and turn often. Barbecuing time varies from 15 to 25 minutes depending on size and weight of meat. Season with salt and pepper.

Squirrel

Squirrel, like rabbit, should be cleaned and cooled quickly. Refrigerate meat about 2 days before barbecuing. Prepare and barbecue squirrel the same as rabbit, but allow a little less time for barbecuing.

Wild Duck

Following basic rules above, refrigerate duck 2 or 3 days before barbecuing. Halve or quarter duck. Brush with cooking oil. Space briquets 1/2 inch apart. Lay duck on grill. Lower grill and sear each side of duck 1 to 2 minutes. Raise grill and barbecue 3 inches above briquets. Brush with melted butter and turn often. Barbecue 10 to 15 minutes or until done as desired. To spit barbecue wild ducks, see page 41.

Venison Steak

HERE IS WHAT YOU NEED

Venison, aged 1 to 3 weeks and cut into steaks about 1 inch thick. Allow 1 steak per person.

A cut clove of garlic, cooking oil, salt and pepper.

Barbecue brush, tongs for handling and turning of steaks.

HERE IS WHAT YOU DO

1 Rub both sides of steaks lightly with garlic. Then, brush steaks with cooking oil.

2 Space hot briquets about 1/2 inch apart.

3 Lay steaks on grill. Lower grill and sear steaks 1 to 2 minutes. Then, raise grill about 3 inches above the briquets; barbecue 5 or 10 minutes on each side for rare- or medium-done steaks. Brush steaks with cooking oil and turn.

4 Lower grill again; sear steaks 1 to 2 minutes. Raise grill and barbecue until steaks are done as desired.

5 Remove from grill and season with salt and pepper.

Rock Lobster Tails

HERE IS WHAT YOU NEED

Rock lobster tails about 1/2 pound each. Allow 2 per person.

Melted butter or margarine, salt, pepper and lemon wedges. Chow Chow Sauce for dunking, if desired (see page 62).

Scissors for slitting shell. Tongs for turning and barbecue brush.

HERE IS WHAT YOU DO

1 Slit underside of lobster shell lengthwise with scissors. Then, bend tail backwards to crack the shell. This prevents curling.

2 Space the hot briquets 1/2 inch apart.

3 Put lobster tails on grill, shell-side down, and barbecue 3 inches above briquets.

4 Barbecue lobster about 15 minutes. Brush with melted butter; turn. Barbecue 3 to 4 minutes longer. The shell is bright red when barbecued.

5 Remove from grill and season with salt and pepper. Serve with lemon wedges, melted butter or Chow Chow Sauce.

Lobsters

Have fresh 1- to 1½-pound lobsters split lengthwise, cleaned and the large claws cracked. Allow 1 lobster per person. Spread lobster open as far as possible. Space the hot briquets 1/2 inch apart. Lay lobsters, shell-side down, on grill; barbecue 3 inches above briquets, about 15 minutes. Brush lobsters with melted butter or margarine; turn. Barbecue about 5 minutes longer. Shell is bright red when lobsters are done. Serve with hot, melted butter or margarine, lemon wedges, salt and pepper.

Grilled Shrimp

Select large green (raw) shrimp. Allow about 1/2 pound per person. If frozen, thaw completely. Remove shell and dark sand vein. Wash shrimp under cold, running water; dry with paper towels. Put shrimp in hand grill; secure handle. Brush both sides of shrimp with melted butter or margarine. Space briquets about 1/2 inch apart. Barbecue shrimp 3 inches above briquets about 4 minutes on each side. Serve with melted butter or Zippy Dunking Sauce (see page 62), if desired.

Barbecued Clams

Buy small, hard-shell clams (littlenecks, cherry stones or butter clams) in shell. Allow about 6 per person. Scrub shells well under running water. Then, soak in cold, salted water about 1 hour to remove sand. Dry with paper towels. Space briquets 1/2 inch apart. Place clams on grill close to briquets. Barbecue about 5 minutes, or until shell opens and clams are heated. Serve with piping hot, melted butter and lemon wedges, if desired. Oysters may also be prepared in the same way.

Oysters In Blankets

Buy fresh or frozen, shucked oysters. Allow about 6 per person. Have oysters at room temperature; drain. Wrap each one in 1/2 slice of bacon; secure with wooden picks. Put in a fine mesh, hand grill; secure handle. Space briquets 1/2 inch apart. Barbecue until bacon is done; turn often.

Small Whole Fish

HERE IS WHAT YOU NEED

Small whole fish (butterfish, bluefish, pike). Allow about 2 fish per person.

Coating for Fish: Make a paste of 1/3 cup flour, 1/4 cup cooking oil, 1/4 teaspoon salt and a dash pepper. Makes enough to coat about 5 fish. Salt and pepper.

Tongs for turning fish. Spatula to remove fish from grill.

HERE IS WHAT YOU DO

1 Dip fish in Coating for Fish.

2 Space hot briquets 1/2 inch apart.

3 Lay fish on grill. Lower grill and sear fish about 1/2 minute. Then, raise grill 3 inches above briquets and barbecue 3 to 4 minutes. Grasp fish by the head with tongs and turn.

4 Lower grill again and sear second side of fish 1/2 minute. Raise grill and continue to barbecue for an additional 3 to 4 minutes.

5 Remove fish from grill with spatula. Season with salt and pepper.

Spit Barbecuing

Spit Barbecuing

Spit barbecuing requires less attention than grill barbecuing and is probably the easiest of all to do. A spit and a motor on your unit permits barbecuing roasts, whole poultry and large whole fish. With the addition of a spit basket, you can also barbecue chops, spareribs, chicken parts and small whole fish. Just follow the step-by-step instructions.

1 Remove the wire grill and on braziers also lift out the raiser rod.

2 Start the fire by one of the methods described on page 7.

3 Place the food on the spit or arrange it in the spit basket.

4 Pile hot briquets, about 3 deep, toward the rear of the fire bowl or fire pan. They must cover an area which will extend beyond the ends of the meat after the spit is attached.

5 Insert the pointed end of the spit rod into the motor. Slip the spit rod bearing into the gravity slot or groove. On units with round spit rods, tighten the screw on the motor to hold the spit rod securely.

6 Place the drip pan under the meat in front of the fire (see page 33). Turn on the motor.

7 To control the heat on brazier units, add or remove briquets (see page 8, item 2); on wagon units, raise or lower the fire pan. Place extra briquets near the fire to warm up. Add the briquets to the fire as needed.

8 Meats are barbecuing when juices bubble on the surface.

9 As foods revolve on the spit, juices come to the surface and baste the food. However, some meats, especially lean ones, require additional basting. Use melted butter or margarine, cooking oil or the natural juices from the drip pan. When using barbecue sauces for basting, apply them only during the last 10 or 15 minutes of barbecuing.

General Rules for the Spit Rod

Put a spit fork on the spit rod near the handle end ⟍ Then insert spit rod into the meat ⟍ (see specific directions on the following pages). Slip second fork on the rod ⟍ Insert forks in the meat ⟍ and slightly tighten the screws. Test for balance ⟍. Reposition meat if it is not balanced or use counter weights (see page 33). Tighten screws with pliers ⟍. The meat must be held securely by the spit forks and the fork screws must be tight.

Easy as 1-2-3

Balance on the Spit

Balance of meat on the spit rod is most important. When the meat is out of balance, as the spit revolves it has a tendency to turn unevenly, putting a strain on the motor.

Before inserting the rod in the roast, estimate the center of balance. Slide the roast to the middle of the rod and partially tighten the fork screws. Holding the spit as shown in the drawing at the right, roll the rod back and forth on the palms of the hands. When properly balanced, it rolls evenly. If it tips or rolls unevenly, it will be necessary to reposition the rod in the meat, or to attach counter weights to the spit. When using counter weights, adjust them until the spit revolves evenly.

The Barbecue Thermometer

A barbecue thermometer is the best guide to tell when a roast is done. Insert the thermometer so the metal tip rests in the center of the thickest part of the meat. It must not touch the spit or bone, or rest in fat.

In the larger birds such as chickens, capons, and turkey the thickest part of the meat, of course, is the area between the thigh and the body. It is not practical to use a thermometer in smaller birds — small chickens, squab, Cornish hens and ducks.

Put the thermometer in the roast before attaching the spit to the motor. Make sure the thermometer stem is not at right angles to the spit rod or it will fall out as the spit turns. Position the thermometer so it will not touch or rub against the briquets, the drip pan or the hood.

When meat is done, lift the spit from the unit. Remove thermometer. Slip meat off rod; let stand 5 to 10 minutes to firm up for easier carving.

Drip Pans and How to Make Them

For all spit barbecuing, you will need a drip pan to catch the juices and fat as they drip from the meat. Use these drippings for basting and to serve with the cooked meat. The pan also prevents the fat from falling on the fire, causing flame-ups and excessive smoke.

To make a pan, use heavy duty aluminum foil 18 inches wide. Tear off a piece 5 inches longer than the meat on the spit and fold it in half, lengthwise. Then, turn the foil up about 1½ inches from each edge and fold or mitre the corners to seal them and make the sides rigid.

Place the pan in front of the burning briquets and under the meat. It may be necessary as barbecuing progresses to change the location of the pan to catch the drippings as they fall.

Spit Barbecuing

TO PUT POULTRY ON THE SPIT

Flatten the wings against the body and tie each bird with heavy twine; loop it around the body several times to hold the wings in place. (If the bird is a turkey or capon, skewer the neck skin to the back, before tying the wings.) Tie the legs and tail together. Put the birds on the spit, one at a time, following General Rules for Using a Spit Rod on page 32. Insert the rod in the neck area. Run it through the bird, parallel to the backbone and bring it out between the tail and legs. Birds can be put on all breast-side up. Or, for better balance, you can alternate them, one breast-side up and the next breast-side down as shown on page 40.

Push the birds together at the center of the rod. Insert the spit forks, at each end of the rod, into the shoulder flesh and the other in the back near the tail. For smaller birds such as Cornish hens and ducks, it may be necessary to bend the tines of the forks together and use additional twine for tying the birds to the forks.

When barbecuing a single bird of any size, or two larger birds at the same time, use a pair of forks for each bird.

Balance the birds on the spit and insert the barbecue thermometer (see page 33).

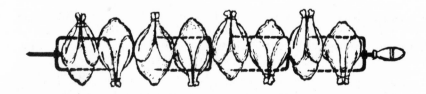

When barbecuing Cornish hens, squab or other very small birds, you can increase the capacity of the spit rod by putting the birds on the rod vertically as shown, above, alternating heads and tails. Use a spit fork for every two birds.

Easy as 1-2-3

BONED ROLLED ROASTS

These instructions are for all the following boned and rolled roasts: Ribs of Beef, Sirloin Tip, Double Loin of Pork, Leg of Lamb and Ham. In addition, use these instructions for Tenderloin of Beef and Smoked Pork Butt.

Have the meat-man tie the roast (except the Beef Tenderloin and Smoked Butt which need no tying) with heavy twine at 1½-inch intervals. If the roast is a beef roast and does not have enough fat on the outside surface, have it wrapped in a thin layer of suet before tying. Following the General Rules for Using the Spit Rod on page 32, insert the spit rod through the center of the roast as shown, at left. Position it at the center of the rod. Balance the roast; insert the barbecue thermometer (see page 33).

RIB ROASTS

Pork Loin Roast An entire loin or just a part of one can be barbecued at one time. When cooking a whole loin, you can have it cut into two or three pieces. This is especially desirable if you plan to use smoke chips. When a loin is cut in several pieces, it will be necessary to have 2 spit forks for each piece.

Put each piece of the roast on the spit rod following the General Rules for Use of the Spit Rod. When all pork is on the rod, balance it and insert the barbecue thermometer (see page 33).

Ribs of Beef You can barbecue as few as two ribs or as many as seven ribs at a time. For best results, the backbone should be left on the roast, but have the meat-man remove the short ribs. It is also best to have rib bones no longer than 7 inches. Following the General Rules for Using the Spit Rod, insert the spit rod in the meat crosswise to the bone and in the center of the muscle, as shown. Position the roast at the center of the rod. Balance the roast and insert the barbecue thermometer (see page 33).

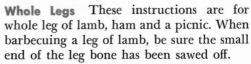

Spit Barbecuing

LEG ROASTS

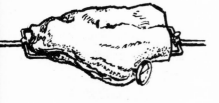

Whole Legs These instructions are for whole leg of lamb, ham and a picnic. When barbecuing a leg of lamb, be sure the small end of the leg bone has been sawed off.

Following General Directions for Using the Spit Rod on page 32, insert the rod in the leg and run it through, lengthwise, as near the center as possible. Because of the joint in the thick part of the leg, it may be necessary to try several times until you get the spit through. Test for balance. Reposition the rod or use counter weights, as necessary. These roasts, especially hams and picnics, are difficult to balance properly without the use of counter weights.

Legs Cut in Half When barbecuing an entire ham, it is easier to balance on the spit if it has been cut in half. Have the meat-man cut the ham diagonally as shown at the left. Put the spit rod through each half, offsetting the shank end, for balance.

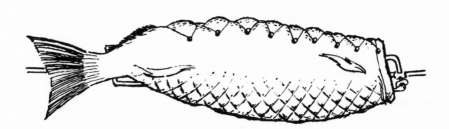

LARGE WHOLE FISH

Have the fish cleaned and head removed. Fasten the body cavity with small metal skewers at 1-inch intervals. Lace securely with heavy twine. Run the spit rod, lengthwise, through the fish. Insert the spit forks at each end, bending the tines, as necessary, to hold the fish in place.

Easy as 1-2-3

Use of the Spit Basket

A spit basket for a barbecue unit is a real boon to the barbecue chef, for it allows him to relax and visit with his guests. Food in the basket revolves constantly over the fire, eliminating the close watching so frequently necessary when barbecuing on the grill. Use it for such foods as chops, spareribs, chicken parts, small whole fish, fish steaks and lobster tails.

Lay the basket on a flat surface and open the cover. Put a spit fork on the spit rod near the handle end; run the rod through loops at the ends of the basket. Slip second fork onto the rod.

Arrange food in the basket, placing it close together. Put the top on the basket, using pressure to engage it under the lowest wires possible on each of the long sides of the basket. Insert spit forks into the food in the basket and tighten the fork screws. Holding the spit rod in the palms of the hands, rotate it. If food slips or shifts, the cover is not on tight enough. It is important that you place the food very close together. If the food is not packed properly and cover is not tight enough, the food will loosen as it cooks and may slide to one side or fall out.

Time required for cooking in the spit basket is a little longer than when cooking on the grill.

CHICKEN HALVES AND QUARTERS

Have meat-man crack the bones so pieces will lay flat in the basket. After cover is in place, brush the chicken on both sides with cooking oil, melted butter or margarine.

SPARERIBS

Cut spareribs apart into individual servings. Arrange ribs in two layers. Put first layer meaty side down and second layer meaty side up. Put cover in place.

ROCK LOBSTER TAILS

Slit the undershell, lengthwise, with scissors and bend the tail backwards to crack the shell. Arrange in the basket, alternating the tail ends. Put cover in place and brush the slit side of lobster with melted butter or margarine. Brush occasionally during barbecuing.

Capons

HERE IS WHAT YOU NEED

Ready-to-cook capons, weighing from 6 to 8 pounds each. Allow 3/4 to 1 pound per person.

Salt, pepper and cooking oil. Melted butter or margarine and Cranberry Glaze (see page 61), if desired.

Spit rod and forks, pliers, heavy twine, barbecue brush, drip pan, barbecue thermometer, cutting board, carving knife and fork.

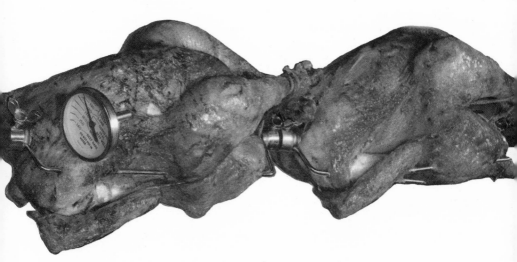

HERE IS WHAT YOU DO

1 Sprinkle body cavity of each capon with 1 to 2 tablespoons salt and a little pepper.

2 Tie birds with twine and put on the spit as directed for poultry on page 34. Brush birds with cooking oil. Insert barbecue thermometer, as shown.

3 Pile hot briquets for spit barbecuing.

4 Attach spit and place drip pan under birds. Turn on the motor.

5 Brush birds with pan drippings or melted butter, frequently during barbecuing. Brush with glaze the last 10 to 15 minutes of barbecuing.

6 Barbecue until done, allowing about 15 minutes per pound or a total of 1½ to 2 hours barbecuing time. Barbecue thermometer should register 190°.

Barbecued Chickens

Use ready-to-cook broiler-fryers or young roasting chickens, weighing from 2 to 3½ pounds. You can barbecue as many as 3 at a time. Allow about 1/2 chicken per person.

With the following exceptions prepare and barbecue broiler-fryers the same way you would Capons on opposite page. Use only 2 to 3 teaspoons salt in body cavity of each chicken. When birds are done, the barbecue thermometer should register 190° the same as for capon. However, because these birds are smaller, they require a shorter cooking period — allow about 20 minutes per pound or only 40 to 70 minutes total barbecuing time.

Barbecued Turkey

HERE IS WHAT YOU NEED

Either a ready-to-cook hen turkey, weighing 8 to 15 pounds, or a ready-to-cook tom turkey, weighing 13 to 18 pounds. Allow about 3/4 pound per person.

Salt and cooking oil. Wine vinegar and hickory smoke chips (see page 48) for added flavor, if desired.

Spit rod and forks, pliers and drip pan. Heavy twine, barbecue thermometer, barbecue brush, cutting board, carving knife and fork.

HERE IS WHAT YOU DO

1 Sprinkle body cavity of turkey with salt, allowing 3 tablespoons salt for a 9-pound bird or about 1 teaspoon salt per pound. Rinse the body cavity with wine vinegar before using salt, if desired.

2 Tie bird with heavy twine and put on the spit as directed for poultry on page 34. Brush with cooking oil. Insert barbecue thermometer (see page 33).

3 Pile hot briquets for spit barbecuing.

4 Attach the spit and place the drip pan under turkey. Turn on the motor.

5 Put hickory smoke chips on the fire and replace as required.

6 Brush turkey often during barbecuing with pan drippings or cooking oil.

7 Barbecue bird until done, allowing about 22 minutes per pound for hen turkeys and about 18 minutes per pound for tom turkeys. But, let the barbecue thermometer be the last word. It should register 190°.

8 When turkey is done, lift out thermometer. Remove bird from spit and let it stand about 10 minutes to firm up before carving.

Barbecued Pheasant

HERE IS WHAT YOU NEED

Ready-to-cook pheasants, weighing about 2 pounds each. Refrigerate 2 or 3 days before barbecuing. (See the basic rules for care of game on page 26.) Allow 1/2 pheasant per person.

Salt, celery leaves, lemon slices, cloves of garlic, bay leaves. Pieces of bacon or salt pork, if desired; cooking oil, melted butter.

Metal skewers, spit rod and forks, heavy twine, barbecue thermometer, drip pan, barbecue brush.

HERE IS WHAT YOU DO

1 Sprinkle body cavities with salt. Put celery, lemon slices, garlic and bay leaves into body cavities; close cavities with skewers and lace with twine. Put bacon on each breast and tie securely.

2 Tie pheasants and put on spit rod as directed for poultry on page 34. If they are plump, insert barbecue thermometer, as shown. Brush pheasants with cooking oil.

3 Pile hot briquets for spit barbecuing.

4 Attach the spit; place drip pan under pheasants. Turn on the motor.

5 During barbecuing, brush pheasants frequently with pan drippings or melted butter. Barbecue until done, allowing 15 to 20 minutes per pound for a medium- or well-done pheasant. Thermometer will register 170° to 190°. Lift out thermometer; remove pheasants from spit. Discard seasonings from body cavities.

Cornish Game Hen

HERE IS WHAT YOU NEED

Rock Cornish game hens, weighing about 1 pound each. Allow 1 hen per person.

Salt and cooking oil. Melted butter and Three Fruit Glaze, if desired (see page 61).

Spit rod and forks, pliers, drip pan. Heavy twine, barbecue brush.

HERE IS WHAT YOU DO

1 Sprinkle 1/2 teaspoon salt in the body cavity of each hen.

2 Tie hens with twine and put on spit as directed for poultry on page 34. Brush hens with cooking oil.

3 Pile hot briquets for spit barbecuing.

4 Attach spit; place drip pan under hens. Turn on the motor.

5 Brush hens often with pan drippings or melted butter during barbecuing. Then, the last 10 minutes of barbecuing, brush with glaze.

6 Barbecue until done, or about 45 minutes.

Wild Duck

HERE IS WHAT YOU NEED

Wild ducks, weighing 2 to 3 pounds each. Refrigerate 2 or 3 days before barbecuing. (See care of game on page 26.) Allow 1/2 large, or 1 small duck per person.

Salt, celery leaves, lemon and onion slices, apple wedges, cooking oil, melted butter or margarine; one of the glazes on page 61, if desired.

Skewers, spit rod and forks, pliers, drip pan. Twine and barbecue brush.

HERE IS WHAT YOU DO

1 Sprinkle inside of each body cavity with salt. Put celery, lemon, onion and apple in each cavity. Close cavities with skewers; lace with twine.

2 Tie ducks and put on spit rod as directed for poultry on page 34. Brush with cooking oil.

3 Pile hot briquets for spit barbecuing.

4 Attach the spit; place drip pan under ducks. Turn on the motor.

5 Brush ducks occasionally with pan drippings or melted butter during barbecuing. Brush with glaze the last 10 minutes of barbecuing.

6 Barbecue until done, allowing about 15 minutes per pound for medium-rare duck and 20 minutes per pound for well-done duck.

Rolled Rib Roast

HERE IS WHAT YOU NEED

Rolled rib roast of beef, weighing at least 4 pounds. Allow about 1/2 pound per person.

Cloves of garlic for fire, if desired.

Spit rod and forks, pliers, barbecue thermometer and drip pan. Cutting board, carving knife and fork.

HERE IS WHAT YOU DO

1 Put the meat on the spit as directed for Rib Roasts on page 35. Insert barbecue thermometer, as shown.

2 Pile hot briquets for spit barbecuing.

3 Attach the spit; place drip pan under meat. Throw garlic on fire. Turn on the motor.

4 Barbecue until done as desired, allowing about 15 minutes per pound. Barbecue thermometer should register 140° for rare, 160° for medium, or 170° for well-done beef.

5 Lift thermometer out of meat. Remove meat from the spit and let it stand about 10 minutes to firm up. Carve and serve immediately.

Serve Honey-Rum Grapefruit (see page 57) as an appetizer and Rolled Rib Roast with your choice of barbecued vegetables as the main course.

Standing Rib Roast of Beef

HERE IS WHAT YOU NEED

Standing rib roast of beef. Allow about 3/4 pound per person.
Spit rod and forks, pliers, barbecue thermometer, drip pan.

HERE IS WHAT YOU DO

1 Put meat on spit (see Rib Roast on page 35). Insert thermometer.

2 Pile hot briquets for spit barbecuing.

3 Attach the spit; place drip pan under meat. Turn on the motor.

4 Barbecue until done as desired, allowing 12 to 15 minutes per pound. Thermometer should register 140° for rare, 160° for medium, or 170° for well done.

Tenderloin or Fillet of Beef

Buy a whole tenderloin or fillet of beef. Since this cut is thicker at one end than the other, you can have rare, medium- and well-done meat at the same time. Allow about 1/2 pound per person. Put meat on spit, as directed for Boned Rolled Roasts on page 35. Barbecue 45 to 60 minutes.

Leg of Lamb

HERE IS WHAT YOU NEED

Leg of lamb, weighing at least 6 pounds, or a boned leg of lamb, weighing at least 4 pounds. Allow 1/2 to 3/4 pound per person.
Cooking oil.
Spit rod and forks, pliers, drip pan, barbecue thermometer and brush.

HERE IS WHAT YOU DO

1 Put the meat on the spit as directed for Leg Roasts on page 36. Brush lamb with cooking oil. Insert thermometer.

2 Pile the hot briquets for spit barbecuing.

3 Attach the spit; place drip pan under meat. Turn on the motor.

4 Barbecue until done, allowing about 30 minutes per pound for well-done lamb. Thermometer should register 170° for medium and 180° for well done.

Barbecued Picnic Ham

HERE IS WHAT YOU NEED

"Fully cooked" picnic or shoulder ham, weighing at least 5 pounds. Allow about 1/2 pound per person.

Tangy Pineapple Glaze (see page 61), if desired.

Small, sharp knife. Spit rod and forks, pliers, counter weights, barbecue thermometer, drip pan, barbecue brush.

HERE IS WHAT YOU DO

1 Using a sharp knife, remove any remaining rind from ham.

2 Put ham on spit as directed for Leg Roasts on page 36. Use counter weights, if necessary, to aid in balancing meat. Insert barbecue thermometer, as shown.

3 Pile hot briquets for spit barbecuing. Attach the spit; place drip pan under meat. Turn on the motor.

4 Brush meat with glaze during the last 10 or 15 minutes of barbecuing.

5 Barbecue until done, allowing about 10 minutes per pound. Barbecue thermometer should register 140°.

Barbecued Whole Ham

Buy a "fully cooked" whole ham, weighing 8 to 12 pounds. Allow about 1/2 pound per person. Using a sharp knife, remove any remaining rind. Score fat, if desired. Put the ham on the spit, as shown on page 36. Insert barbecue thermometer. Pile hot briquets for spit barbecuing. Attach the spit; place drip pan under ham. Turn on the motor. If desired, brush ham with one of the glazes on page 61 during the last 10 minutes of barbecuing time. Barbecue until done, allowing about 10 minutes per pound or until barbecue thermometer registers 140°.

A "fully cooked" boned, rolled ham may also be barbecued. Remove the casing. Tie with heavy twine and put on spit as directed for Boned Rolled Roasts on page 35. Barbecue until done, allowing about 10 minutes per pound or until barbecue thermometer registers 140°.

Barbecued Pork Butts

Buy smoked pork butts, weighing about 3 pounds each. Allow about 1/3 pound per person. Remove any casing on meat. Put the meat on the spit rod as directed for Boned Rolled Roasts on page 35. If meat is lean, insert barbecue thermometer. Pile hot briquets for spit barbecuing. Attach the spit; place drip pan under meat. Turn on the motor. If desired, brush meat with one of the glazes on page 61 during the last 10 or 15 minutes of barbecuing. Barbecue until done, allowing 35 minutes per pound, or until barbecue thermometer registers 170°. When meat is done, lift out thermometer. Remove meat from spit and carve.

Spit Barbecued Spareribs

Buy meaty spareribs, allowing about 1 pound of ribs per person. Leave the ribs in one piece for spit barbecuing. Put spareribs on spit rod as follows. Starting at the narrow end of the ribs, run the rod through the middle, lacing the ribs on the rod between the bones. Next, lace the second rack on the rod starting at the wide end, to balance the ribs on the rod. Continue as above until all the ribs are on the rod. Insert spit forks and tighten. Then, run several metal skewers through the ribs, on the outer edges, to hold them securely.

Pile hot briquets for spit barbecuing. Attach the spit; place drip pan under meat. Turn on the motor. Brush meat with one of the glazes on page 61 during the last 10 or 15 minutes of barbecuing time. Barbecue until done. Pork should be barbecued to the well-done stage. Allow 45 minutes to 1 hour total barbecuing time. When ribs are done, meat pulls away from the bones.

Double Pork Loin

HERE IS WHAT YOU NEED

Two pork loins, boned and tied together at 1½-inch intervals and weighing a total of at least 5 pounds. Allow about 1/2 pound per person.

One of the glazes from page 61, if desired.

Spit rod and forks, pliers, barbecue thermometer, drip pan, barbecue brush, cutting board, carving knife and fork.

HERE IS WHAT YOU DO

1 Put pork on spit as directed for Boned Rolled Roasts on page 35. Insert barbecue thermometer, as shown.

2 Pile hot briquets for spit barbecuing.

3 Attach the spit and place drip pan under the meat. Turn on the motor.

4 Brush pork with glaze during the last 10 or 15 minutes of barbecuing time, if desired.

5 Barbecue pork until done, allowing about 20 minutes per pound. Barbecue thermometer should register 190°; meat will be whitish in color when cut.

6 Lift barbecue thermometer out of the meat. Remove meat from the spit and let it stand about 10 minutes to firm up before carving.

Serve with Barbecued Apple Slices (see page 56) and Zippy Lima Beans (see page 55), if desired.

Large Whole Fish

HERE IS WHAT YOU NEED

Large whole fish (salmon, pike, striped bass, bluefish, large mackerel or weakfish), weighing at least 3 pounds. Have fish cleaned and head removed.

Cooking oil and salt. Melted butter or margarine, if desired.

Spit rod and forks, pliers and drip pan. Small métal skewers, heavy twine, barbecue brush.

HERE IS WHAT YOU DO

1 Wash fish thoroughly and dry with paper towels. Brush cavity with cooking oil; sprinkle with salt.

2 Close body cavity with skewers and twine. Put fish on the spit as directed for Large Whole Fish on page 36. Brush fish with cooking oil.

3 Pile hot briquets for spit barbecuing. Attach the spit and place the drip pan under fish. Turn on the motor.

4 Brush fish often during barbecuing with pan drippings, cooking oil or melted butter.

5 Barbecue fish 20 to 40 minutes, or until fish flakes with a fork.

Small Whole Fish

HERE IS WHAT YOU NEED

Small whole fish (mullet, brook trout, snappers, flounder, butterfish or porgies), weighing no more than 2 pounds each. Have fish cleaned and heads and tails removed. Allow 1 fish per person.

Cooking oil. Melted butter or margarine, if desired.

Spit basket, spit rod and forks, pliers, drip pan, barbecue brush.

HERE IS WHAT YOU DO

1 Wash fish thoroughly and dry with paper towels.

2 Following directions for Use of the Spit Basket on page 37, put fish in basket in a single layer. Place them close together and alternate head and tail ends. Adjust the basket cover, being sure it is not too tight or it will tear the skin. Brush fish with cooking oil or melted butter.

3 Pile hot briquets for spit barbecuing. Attach the spit and place the drip pan under spit basket. Turn on the motor.

4 Barbecue fish 10 to 15 minutes, depending upon thickness. Brush during the last 5 minutes with more cooking oil or melted butter.

How to Smoke

Smoking, as you barbecue, introduces an interesting way to change the flavor and character of food. Nut and fruit woods, such as hickory and apple, are used for smoking. The most popular is hickory wood. It is available in several forms including chips and sawdust. Select the flavor and form of wood you desire and smoke-barbecue, using the instructions below.

GENERAL DIRECTIONS

To prepare chips or sawdust for smoking, follow the directions on the package. Generally speaking, chips should be soaked at least 20 minutes before using. Sawdust usually needs only to be moistened.

When using chips, put several soaked chips on the fire just before barbecuing. As chips become hot, they smoke and eventually dry out and burn. When they begin to burn, remove them from the fire with tongs and drop in water; replace with more soaked chips.

When using moistened sawdust, press it into balls or mounds and place on the hot briquets with tongs or a shovel. As sawdust burns, replace with more moistened sawdust.

GRILL SMOKING

Put prepared chips or sawdust on the fire after the gray ash has been knocked off the briquets. Then, barbecue the food on the grill as directed in the recipe.

The smoke penetration of the food can be increased in one of the following ways: One way is to put a larger quantity of smoke chips or sawdust on the fire. Another way is to raise the grill an inch or two above the specified height in the recipe to slow the cooking process. The use of the smoker hood also increases smoke penetration.

Easy as 1-2-3

SPIT SMOKING

Put prepared chips or sawdust on the fire before the spit is attached to the motor. When using the smoker hood, the smoke and heat are confined and food will take on a more pronounced smoke flavor. It will also barbecue faster, so when using a hood, allow about 5 minutes less barbecuing time per pound than specified in the recipes. The use of a smoker hood, the quantity of chips or sawdust used and the length of time the food is smoked, all help determine the amount of smoke penetration.

Of course, the easiest way to control the amount of smoke flavor when grilling or spit barbecuing is with the use of a smoker hood.

WHAT TO SMOKE

What to smoke is a matter of taste. Of course, most all meats, fish, poultry and game can be smoked. Often a slight smoke flavor will give a gourmet's touch to the most simple barbecued food.

Generally speaking, foods which are the most adaptable to smoke cookery are those which contain a lot of fat. Some of these foods are turkey, duck, pork loin, spareribs and fish such as salmon and whitefish.

If you are an enthusiast for heavily smoked meats, you can intensify the smoke flavor of hams, smoked pork butts and picnics with additional smoking.

Try smoking some of the foods mentioned above, then experiment with other foods and let your taste be your guide as to what to smoke.

Salads

Fruit Platter

Salads made of fresh, frozen and canned fruits are an appetizing addition to any barbecue. Fruits can be arranged in several ways. One way is to cut fruits in wedges or spears to serve as finger food. Fruits to use are pineapples, bananas, peaches, apricots, apples and melons. Garnish the platter with salad greens. Serve dressing in little bowls for those who like to dunk the fruit.

A mix-your-own salad is another way to serve fruit. On a platter, arrange a variety of the following: melon balls, cubed pineapple, sliced bananas, peaches and pears. For this type of platter, have a large bowl of salad greens and mayonnaise or fruit salad dressing.

Tossed Green Salad

Select several greens such as lettuce, escarole, romaine, chicory, watercress, young spinach leaves and celery tops. Wash the greens; drain well. Snip or tear them in bite-size pieces. Chill until crisp. Prepare about 2 quarts of greens for 6 servings. Just before serving, put greens in a large bowl; pour about 1/3 cup French Dressing over the top. Toss lightly.

French Dressing

In a pint-size, screw-top jar, put **1/4 cup wine vinegar, 3/4 cup olive oil, 1 teaspoon salt, 1/4 teaspoon black pepper** and **3/4 teaspoon paprika.** Add one or more of the following in a quantity to suit your taste: Tabasco sauce, mustard, curry powder, sugar, garlic, minced chives, thinly sliced raw mushrooms, anchovy paste, sour cream, crumbled blue cheese. Cover jar; shake vigorously. Shake again before using. Makes 1 cup.

Tossed Green Salad

Fruit Platter

Rancher's Salad

4 cups cooked elbow macaroni, chilled	Salt and pepper, to taste
1 can (1 pound) kidney beans, drained	Few drops Tabasco sauce
4 frankfurters, sliced thin	1 tablespoon prepared horse-
1/2 cup sour cream	radish
1/2 cup chili sauce	1 teaspoon prepared mustard
1/2 cup mayonnaise	1 teaspoon Worcestershire sauce

Combine macaroni, beans and frankfurters in a large bowl. Combine all remaining ingredients. Pour over the macaroni mixture. Toss until thoroughly mixed. Turn into a bowl lined with crisp salad greens. Makes 8 servings.

Rice-Vegetable Salad

4 cups hot cooked rice	2 tablespoons minced onion
1/4 cup French dressing	3/4 teaspoon curry powder
1 cup diced celery	Salt and pepper, to taste
1½ cups cooked peas	Few drops Tabasco sauce
3/4 cup mayonnaise	1/2 teaspoon dry mustard

Combine rice and French dressing in a large bowl and allow it to cool. Then, add celery and peas to the rice. Combine remaining ingredients. Pour over rice and vegetables. Toss with a fork. Chill well. Turn into a large bowl lined with salad greens. Garnish with tomato wedges, if desired. Makes 6 servings.

Rice-Vegetable Salad

Rancher's Salad

Barbecued

Slim Jims

Lay **packaged bread sticks** on a double thickness of heavy duty aluminum foil. Melt about **1/4 cup butter or margarine;** season to taste with **a few drops Tabasco sauce** and **a dash of paprika.** Add **1 clove garlic, minced;** stir to mix well. Brush bread sticks with butter mixture. Bring foil up tightly around the bread sticks. Barbecue Slim Jims 5 to 6 minutes on top of the grill, or 3 to 4 minutes on top of the hot briquets; turn the Slim Jims frequently.

Party French Bread

Cut **a long loaf of French bread** diagonally in 1½-inch slices, without cutting clear through. Spread **Mustard Butter** (see page 53) in the diagonal cuts and insert **a half slice of processed American cheese** in each cut. Wrap bread tightly in a single thickness of heavy duty aluminum foil and lay on grill. Heat 20 to 25 minutes, turning often. To make bread more crisp unwrap a few minutes before serving.

Breads

Savory Buns

Mix **canned deviled ham spread** with **a little mayonnaise, a few drops Worcestershire sauce, a dash pepper** and **some chopped parsley.** Spread mixture on **split hamburger buns** and put buns together. Wrap, 2 at a time, in a single thickness of heavy duty aluminum foil and lay on grill. Heat 10 minutes, turning once.

Seasoned Butters

MUSTARD BUTTER

Soften **1/2 cup butter or margarine.** Add and stir in **2 teaspoons prepared mustard** and **a few drops Worcestershire sauce.**

GARLIC BUTTER

Soften **1/2 cup butter or margarine.** Crush **a peeled clove of garlic;** add and stir into butter. Add **a little celery seed,** if desired.

HERB BUTTER

Soften **1/2 cup butter or margarine.** Add and stir in **1 teaspoon thyme or 1 teaspoon rosemary** and **a few drops wine vinegar.**

ROQUEFORT BUTTER

Soften **1/2 cup butter or margarine.** Add and stir in **2 to 3 tablespoons crumbled Roquefort cheese.**

California Beans

Drain contents of **1 can (15½ ounces) whole or cut green beans.** Add **1/2 cup chopped walnuts or blanched slivered almonds, salt and pepper** to taste; toss to mix well. Divide into individual portions and lay each on a double thickness of heavy duty aluminum foil. Top each portion with **a little butter or margarine** and wrap tightly in the foil. Heat on the grill about 20 minutes, turning once, or on top of the briquets 8 to 10 minutes, turning often. Makes 4 to 5 servings.

Thawed, frozen cut beans may also be barbecued on the briquets. Heat about 10 minutes; turn often.

Candied Sweet Potatoes

For each serving, make a rectangle of a double thickness of heavy duty aluminum foil. In the center of each rectangle put **1 canned whole sweet potato,** cut in half, lengthwise; lay cutside up. Place **several orange wedges** on top of each potato, as shown at left. Sprinkle generously with **dark brown sugar** and **cinnamon.** Season with **salt** and **pepper** to taste. Dot with **butter or margarine.** Wrap sweet potato securely in the aluminum foil, being sure to keep the orange wedges on top.

Knock the gray ash off briquets and barbecue the sweet potatoes 10 minutes on the briquets or 30 minutes on the grill; turn potatoes several times.

Vegetables

Zippy Lima Beans

Put the partially thawed contents of **1 package (10 ounces) frozen lima beans** on a double thickness of heavy duty aluminum foil. Slice **1 medium-size onion;** separate into rings and put with lima beans. Add **1/2 cup Zippy Dunking Sauce** (see page 62) and toss to mix well. Wrap the aluminum foil securely around the food.

Knock the gray ash off the briquets. Place aluminum foil wrapped food on the briquets and barbecue 15 to 20 minutes, turning frequently.

For individual servings of Zippy Limas, prepare the beans as above and then divide them into 3 or 4 portions. Wrap each portion securely in aluminum foil and barbecue.

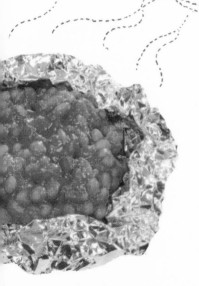

Barbecued Baked Beans

For each person, place **1/2 cup canned Boston-style baked beans** on a double thickness of heavy duty aluminum foil. Then, add and mix in **1 tablespoon Zippy Dunking Sauce** (see page 62). Wrap the foil securely around the beans.

Knock the gray ash off the hot briquets. Lay the foil-wrapped beans on the briquets. Barbecue about 5 minutes, turning once. To grill barbecue beans, place foil-wrapped beans on the grill 3 inches above the briquets. Barbecue about 10 minutes, turning once.

Variation Substitute 2 tablespoons of crushed pineapple for the Zippy Dunking Sauce. Wrap in foil and barbecue.

Barbecued

Barbecued Apple Slices

Select **red-skinned baking apples,** allowing 1 apple per person. Core apples and cut into 1/2-inch wedges. Place individual servings of unpeeled wedges on double thicknesses of heavy duty aluminum foil. Top each serving with **chopped black walnuts.** Sprinkle with **a little sugar, lemon juice, grated lemon peel, nutmeg** and **ginger.** Then, dot with **butter or margarine.**

Knock the gray ash off the briquets. Lay the foil-wrapped wedges on top of the hot briquets or on the grill. Barbecue about 10 minutes on the briquets, turning frequently, or about 30 minutes on the grill, turning several times.

Barbecued Bananas

Peel **firm ripe bananas.** Allow 1 banana per person. Place 1 or 2 bananas on a double thickness of heavy duty aluminum foil and brush with **lemon juice.** Sprinkle generously with **dark brown sugar;** dot with **butter or margarine.** Wrap the foil securely around the bananas.

Knock the gray ash off the briquets. Lay foil-wrapped bananas on briquets and barbecue 7 to 9 minutes; turn frequently. To grill barbecue, lay the foil-wrapped bananas on the grill and barbecue 14 to 17 minutes, 3 inches above briquets; turn frequently. To serve, open aluminum foil and garnish bananas with **red currant jelly** and **a little shredded coconut.**

Fruits

Honey-Rum Grapefruit

Cut **grapefruit** in half, crosswise. Remove the seeds. Cut out the core and loosen each section from the membrane with a sharp pointed knife. In the center of each half, pour **1 tablespoon rum.** Then, top with **a little honey** and sprinkle with **mace.** Wrap each grapefruit half securely in a double thickness of heavy duty aluminum foil.

Knock the gray ash off the briquets and lay grapefruit halves, cut-side up, on top of hot briquets or on the grill. Barbecue about 10 minutes on the briquets or about 20 minutes on the grill. Unwrap grapefruit and serve immediately.

Ginger-Mint Pears

For each individual serving, drain **2 canned pear halves.** Lay pears, cut-side up, on a double thickness of heavy duty aluminum foil.

Put **several pieces of coarsely chopped, crystallized ginger** and **a little apple-mint jelly** in the center of each half. Wrap pears in foil, cut-side up to keep ginger and jelly in place.

Knock gray ash off the briquets and lay foil-wrapped pears, cut-side up, on the briquets or on the grill. Barbecue about 5 minutes on the hot briquets or about 12 minutes on the grill. Unwrap pears and serve immediately.

Desserts

Here are a few things to remember when planning dessert. Have it complement the menu; prepare as much as possible in advance. The desserts on these pages vary from simple cookies for a kiddies' party to Strawberry Pie for a Sunday sit-down dinner out-of-doors.

Short Cake

Short cake may be made from your own recipe, biscuit mix, cake mix or packaged cake. Choose the fruit from the wide variety of fresh and frozen fruits available. Be sure to garnish with lots of whipped cream!

Cookies

The bake shops always have a wide assortment of cookies, if you don't want to bake. Ginger snaps, hermits, toll house and refrigerator cookies are just a few to choose from. They are excellent for the kiddies, because they are not too rich and are easy to handle. Adults will like this simple dessert too!

Cake

Cake is tops with everyone, served plain, with ice cream or with a special frosting. To make the frosting for our gala cake, use sweetened whipped cream and flavor with lemon extract. Then, fold in drained, canned fruit cocktail. Fill and frost cake layers and garnish with additional fruit.

Strawberry Pie

This is a pie for show and for taste. Fill a **baked 9-inch pie shell** with **vanilla pudding** made from a mix, if you like. Cool and cover with this glaze: Hull **1 quart strawberries.** Crush 1 cup of the berries; put in a pan with **3/4 cup sugar** and **1/3 cup water.** Bring to a boil; stir and cook 5 minutes. Mix **1/3 cup water** with **2 tablespoons cornstarch;** stir into berries. Cook and stir until thick and clear. Cool. Fold in remaining berries. Spoon over pie. Chill. Just before serving, garnish with **sweetened whipped cream** and **sliced bananas.**

Cup Cakes

This easy-to-prepare dessert rates high with the small fry. Why not have a large platter of cup cakes topped with a variety of frostings — chocolate, vanilla and lemon? Garnish each cake with a Maraschino cherry or walnut.

Ice Cream Desserts

On hot summer days, cooling ice cream is mighty popular. Whether you buy it or make it yourself, be sure to have plenty on hand for those who want seconds. And there is no end of ways to serve it. Just plain ice cream — any flavor — is the simplest. Or, have several pitchers of sundae syrups, bowls of nuts and whipped cream for guests to make their own concoctions. When you want an elegant ice cream dessert, make cantaloupe coupes. Allow a half cantaloupe for each serving; arrange 4 banana wedges in each and anchor them with a scoop of ice cream.

From Marinades to Relishes

Marinades, sauces, glazes and relishes — these are the extras which work magic on the simplest barbecue fare, turning it into food fit for a king. When using these extras, remember these facts.

Marinades tenderize and give flavor to meat before cooking.

Basting sauces keep meat moist during cooking and give it a subtle flavor.

Glazes make meats mouth-watering to look at as well as to eat.

Relishes and sauces for dunking add color and zest to any barbecue.

Speedy Marinade

Combine **1/4 teaspoon rosemary, 1/4 teaspoon tarragon, 1/4 teaspoon thyme** and **1/4 cup cooking oil** in a saucepan. Heat and stir over low heat. Add **1/2 cup lemon juice.** Remove from heat. Pour marinade over meat. Cover and let stand several hours at room temperature; turn meat several times. Lift meat out of marinade before barbecuing and save the marinade. Brush meat with marinade during barbecuing, if desired.

Good with chicken, beef and lamb.

Spiced Marinade

1/2 cup water	2 tablespoons minced onion
1/2 cup wine vinegar	2 bay leaves
1/2 cup cooking oil	4 whole cloves

Combine all ingredients in a bowl. Stir to mix well. Pour marinade over meat; cover and let stand in refrigerator about 4 hours, turning once. Lift meat out of the marinade before barbecuing and save the marinade. Brush meat with marinade during barbecuing, if desired.

Good with beef, lamb and chicken.

Mint Marinade

Combine **1 cup prepared mint sauce** and **2/3 cup cooking oil.** Pour marinade over meat. Cover and let stand at room temperature about 3 hours, turning meat once. Lift meat out of marinade before barbecuing. Save marinade and brush meat with it during barbecuing, if desired.

Good with lamb or beef.

Sweet-Sour Basting Sauce

3 tablespoons cooking oil
1½ teaspoons salt
3 tablespoons minced green pepper
3/4 cup wine vinegar
1 can (6 ounces) thawed, frozen pineapple
    juice concentrate
1/2 cup dark brown sugar
1½ teaspoons soy sauce

Put all the ingredients in a saucepan. Simmer
over low heat 15 minutes, stirring often. Brush
meat with sauce often during the last 10 to 15 minutes of barbecuing.
Makes enough for 3 large pieces of meat.

Good with spareribs, chops or ham. Use it also as a sauce for dunking.

Cranberry Glaze

Combine **1 cup mashed, jellied cranberry sauce, 1/3 cup firmly packed
brown sugar, 1/4 teaspoon mace** and **1/4 teaspoon cinnamon.** Brush
meat often with glaze during last 10 minutes of barbecuing. Enough glaze
for 3 chickens.

Good with pork, ham or chicken.

Three Fruit Glaze

1 large fully-ripe banana, mashed	1 tablespoon lemon juice
1/4 cup thawed, frozen orange juice concentrate	1/4 cup light corn syrup
	1/8 teaspoon cinnamon

Combine all ingredients in a bowl. Brush meat often with glaze during the
last 10 to 15 minutes of barbecuing. Enough glaze for 3 birds.

Good with pheasant or duck, chicken and cornish game hens.

Tangy Pineapple Glaze

Combine **1/2 cup thawed, frozen pineapple juice concentrate, 3 tablespoons wine vinegar, 1/4 cup water, 1/3 cup brown sugar** and **1 teaspoon ginger** in a saucepan. Heat and stir until sugar dissolves. Baste meat
often with glaze during the last 5 to 15 minutes of barbecuing time. Makes
enough glaze for 1 large piece of meat.

Good with pork, ham or any fruit kebobs.

Zippy Dunking Sauce

2/3 cup chili sauce
2/3 cup tomato catchup
1½ teaspoons minced onion
1 tablespoon tarragon vinegar
1 small clove garlic, peeled
2 tablespoons lemon juice
1/2 teaspoon salt
Dash pepper
Dash cayenne

Measure all ingredients into a screw-top jar. Cover tightly and shake to mix well. Chill at least 1 to 2 hours to blend the flavors. Remove garlic before serving. Makes about 1½ cups sauce.

Good with steak, hot dogs, hamburgers, or as a dip for seafood.

Chow Chow Sauce

1 can (6 ounces) tomato paste
1 teaspoon dry mustard
1/4 cup brown sugar
1 teaspoon salt
Few grains chili powder
1 tablespoon Worcestershire sauce
1 medium-size onion, minced
1/4 cup wine vinegar
2 tablespoons water
2 teaspoons lemon juice

Combine all ingredients in a saucepan. Heat to boiling, stirring occasionally. Remove from heat; let stand several hours at room temperature to blend the flavors before serving.

Good with steak, chops, spareribs, hamburgers, hot dogs and any fish or seafood.

Mustard Sauce

Combine **1 cup sour cream, 4 tablespoons prepared mustard, 1 tablespoon minced onion, 1/2 teaspoon salt** and **a dash pepper** in a small saucepan. Blend thoroughly. Warm over low heat. Makes 1 cup sauce.

Good with pork, ham or as a dip for seafood.

Cucumber Relish

1½ cups finely chopped cucumber
1/2 cup grated carrot
1/4 cup minced onion
2 teaspoons salt
1/4 cup wine vinegar
1/2 teaspoon dill seed

Combine all ingredients in a bowl. Toss to mix well. Chill in refrigerator overnight to blend flavors. Makes about 2 cups relish.

Good with steak, hamburgers or your favorite fish or seafood.

Printed by Brett Litho Co., L. I. C. 1, N.